Fats, Oils, and Sweets

by Helen Frost

Consulting Editor: Gail Saunders-Smith, Ph.D.

Consultant: Linda Hathaway
Health Educator
McMillen Center for Health Education

Pebble Books

an imprint of Capstone Press
Mankato, Minnesota

Pebble Books are published by Capstone Press
151 Good Counsel Drive, P.O. Box 669, Mankato, Minnesota 56002
http://www.capstone-press.com

1 2 3 4 5 6 05 04 03 02 01 00

Library of Congress Cataloging-in-Publication Data
Frost, Helen, 1949–
    Fats, oils, and sweets/by Helen Frost.
    p. cm.—(The food guide pyramid)
    Includes bibliographical references and index.
    Summary: Simple text and photographs show fats, oils, and sugary foods, and
explain how you can make healthy food choices.
    ISBN 0-7368-0536-2
    1. Oils and fats—Juvenile literature. 2. Nutrition—Juvenile literature.
3. Confectionery—Juvenile literature. [1. Oils and fats. 2. Nutrition. 3. Sugar.]
I. Title. II. Series.
TX560.F3F76   2000
613.2′84—dc21   99-056381

Note to Parents and Teachers

The Food Guide Pyramid series supports national science standards related to physical health and nutrition. This book describes and illustrates fats, oils, and sweets. The photographs support early readers in understanding the text. The repetition of words and phrases helps early readers learn new words. This book also introduces early readers to subject-specific vocabulary words, which are defined in the Words to Know section. Early readers may need assistance to read some words and to use the Table of Contents, Words to Know, Read More, Internet Sites, and Index/Word List sections of the book.

Table of Contents

4

The food guide pyramid shows the foods you need to stay healthy. Fats, oils, and sweets are at the top of the food guide pyramid.

Fat is found in animals and in some plants. Butter is a solid fat. Oil is made from the fat in plants. Oil is a liquid fat.

Sweets are foods that have a lot of sugar. Candy is a sweet. Sweets give you energy. But the energy does not last long.

Fats, oils, and sweets
do not have many of
the nutrients you need.
You can choose foods
that do not have much
fat, oil, and sugar.

You can choose orange juice instead of soda pop. Orange juice has less sugar than soda pop.

You can choose pretzels instead of potato chips. Pretzels have less fat than potato chips.

You can choose a bagel instead of a donut. A bagel has less fat and less sugar than a donut.

You can put lemon juice on your salad. Lemon juice has less oil than salad dressing.

Fats, oils, and sweets are not healthy foods. You should eat only a small amount of fats, oils, and sweets.

Words to Know

energy—the strength to be active without becoming tired

fat—an oily substance found in the bodies of animals and some plants; meat, nuts, and some dairy products have fat.

food guide pyramid—a triangle split into six areas to show the different foods you need to eat to stay healthy

nutrient—something that people, plants, and animals need to stay healthy; fats, oils, and sweets do not have many of the nutrients you need to stay healthy.

oil—a liquid made from the fat in plants; oils are found in foods such as peanuts and soybeans.

sugar—a sweet substance that comes from plants; some foods have sugar.

sweet—a food that has a lot of sugar; sweets give you energy that does not last long.

Read More

Frost, Helen. *Eating Right.* The Food Guide Pyramid. Mankato, Minn.: Pebble Books, 2000.

Frost, Helen. *Food for Healthy Teeth.* Dental Health. Mankato, Minn.: Pebble Books, 1999.

Kalbacken, Joan. *The Food Pyramid.* A True Book. New York: Children's Press, 1998.

Rockwell, Lizzy. *Good Enough to Eat: A Kid's Guide to Food and Nutrition.* New York: HarperCollins, 1999.

Internet Sites

The ABCs of Fats, Oils, and Cholesterol
http://www.eatright.org/nfs/nfs2.html

Food Pyramid Guide: The Easy Way to Eat Right!
http://www.ganesa.com/food

Healthy Food Choices
http://www.ama-assn.org/insight/h_focus/
nemours/nutritio/child612/choices.htm

Index/Word List

Word Count: 190
Early-Intervention Level: 13

Editorial Credits
Mari C. Schuh, editor; Heather Kindseth, cover designer; Sara A. Sinnard, illustrator; Kia Bielke, illustrator; Kimberly Danger, photo researcher

Photo Credits
David F. Clobes, 12, 14, 16, 18, 20
Gregg R. Andersen, cover, 6, 8
Lora Askinazi/Index Stock Imagery, 10
Photo Network/Dede Gilman, 1